ABANDONED JACKSONVILLE

REMNANTS OF THE RIVER CITY

DAVID BULIT

AMERICA
THROUGH TIME®
ADDING COLOR TO AMERICAN HISTORY

America Through Time is an imprint of Fonthill Media LLC
www.through-time.com
office@through-time.com

Published by Arcadia Publishing by arrangement with Fonthill Media LLC
For all general information, please contact Arcadia Publishing:
Telephone: 843-853-2070
Fax: 843-853-0044
E-mail: sales@arcadiapublishing.com
For customer service and orders:
Toll-Free 1-888-313-2665

www.arcadiapublishing.com

First published 2020

ISBN 978-1-63499-243-5

Typeset in Trade Gothic 10pt on 15pt
Printed and bound in England

CONTENTS

ABOUT THE AUTHOR

David Bulit is a Hialeah native, a city within the greater Miami area, who has spent nearly a decade documenting abandoned locales throughout the state of Florida. Mostly known for his blog, Abandoned Florida, his photography has been featured by local, national, and international news outlets. His other published works include *Abandoned Jacksonville: Ruins of the First Coast, Lost Miami: Stories and Secrets of Magic City Ruins* and *Southern Comfort: Abandoned Homes of the American South.*

INTRODUCTION

When I wrote and photographed *Abandoned Jacksonville*, I had no idea that it would be so popular and gain as much traction as it did. For a while, Jacksonville felt like a second home for me due to the number of times I visited the city in the past few years. I've seen the city from up above the old JEA tower, and I've been beneath it, not only in the bank vaults and basements of the Barnett Bank and Marble Bank, but also in the flooded tunnels of the Jacksonville Terminal. The second and last volume of the series contains even more places that I couldn't fit in the first book and I hope you find them as exciting as I did.

I've since moved on to expand my horizons beyond Florida, but it doesn't mean that my work in Florida will end. Florida will always be my home and I intend to continue exploring the state. I have other ideas for books I wish to complete, and that doesn't include the ones already being worked on, such as one involving abandoned places in Montgomery, Alabama.

Thank you all for continuing to support me and for coming out for my book signing. With that, I'd like to thank Chamblin's Uptown in downtown Jacksonville for allowing me to have a signing there, as I had such a wonderful experience. I would also like to thank Tim Gilmore, who continues to tell the lesser-known stories of Jacksonville and for inspiring me on numerous occasions. To all my friends, thank you, as I know this has been a crazy and hectic year and I appreciate the patience you've had with me. I hope you all enjoy this book as much as I enjoyed photographing these places and putting it together.

1

JACKSONVILLE TERMINAL PASSENGER TUNNELS

As early as 1890, Henry Flagler, owner of the Florida East Coast Railway, began purchasing property, mostly marshland just west of Jacksonville. In 1894, Flagler organized the Jacksonville Terminal Company with ownership being split between five railroad companies: Atlantic Coast Line Railroad, Florida East Coast Railway, and Seaboard Air Line Railway, each with 25% ownership, and Southern Railway and Georgia Southern and Florida Railway each with 12.5% ownership. Its first Union Depot opened on February 4, 1895, and was completed on January 15, 1897. It later became known as Flagler Depot.

Built on the site of the original one, a new Union Station opened in 1919 and at the time, it was the largest railroad station in the South. At its peak, the terminal handled as many as 142 trains and 20,000 passengers a day. Some of the passenger trains handled in Jacksonville were eighteen to twenty-two railcars long. Within the terminal, there was a restaurant, snack bars, newsstands, a barbershop, a florist, a drug store, and gift shops. The Jacksonville terminal had thirty-two tracks. Twenty-nine of those tracks were passenger tracks with platforms.

The station was last used on January 3, 1974; Amtrak moved to a new Jacksonville station several miles north. The station was abandoned until 1982, when a public-private partnership was started, led by former CSX chairman Prime F. Osborn III. The building reopened on October 17, 1986, as the Prime F. Osborn III Convention Center.

Even though the station has since been renovated, the tunnels, which were built to bring passengers safely under the platforms to board trains on far tracks, have been buried and forgotten. Each platform had its own ramp which connected with the main tunnel and led to the main building. For the most part, the tunnels remain intact and are currently filled with 3-4 feet of water, roaches, rats, and various other critters.

Above: The historic Jacksonville Terminal

Left: Glowsticks illuminate the dark tunnels

The tunnels are flooded with around 3-4 feet of water

The main atrium for the tunnels

Above: An old signpost can be seen in the top left

Left: Looking down at the entrance I came through

Right: My girlfriend illuminating the tunnels with a lantern

Below: The entrances to the tunnels have since been buried

2

MT. CALVARY BAPTIST CHURCH

The Mount Calvary Baptist Church is a church located in the historically black neighborhood of Brooklyn. Originally known as Dell's Bluff when it was first settled in 1801, the Brooklyn neighborhood was originally home to a sprawling, 800-acre plantation owned by Phillip Dell. The property changed hands several times before the American Civil War. Following the war, it was purchased by Miles Price, a Confederate veteran, who sold off the southern portion of the property to be developed as Riverside. The northern portion he developed himself would later become Brooklyn.

While Price was the one to name the neighborhood, it's not known why a former Confederate chose a name associated with the New York borough of Brooklyn. The west and east streets, however, would be named after Confederate generals. The north and south streets are named after trees. The area was developed as a residential suburb and quickly grew after the establishment of a streetcar line.

Many African-American former soldiers, known as Buffalo Soldiers, settled down in Brooklyn. By the 1880s, it held a population of 1,000 and a few hundred homes and mansions. In 1887, Brooklyn and several other suburbs were annexed by Jacksonville.

By the 1950s, the neighborhood had nearly 6,000 residents. The neighborhood remained primarily residential, but it eventually developed into a commercial and industrial area due to the increasing use of the railway. Construction of the Fuller Warren Bridge cut off the historically black neighborhood, pushing many of the residents out. This slowly led to the decline of the neighborhood, leaving many of the remaining structures in disrepair, such as the Buffalo Soldier's House.

The Mount Calvary Baptist Church was abandoned in 1999, but before then it served the community for many decades. The building was built in 1955 by James Edwards Hutchins, one of the few black architects/builders during this era, and was commissioned by the church under the leadership of Reverend William Hill.

James Edward Hutchins was born on November 25, 1890, in Blakeley, Georgia, and moved to Jacksonville after completing his studies at the Savannah state college. Hutchins is recognized as one of the few African-American contractors in Jacksonville who designed as well as built. As a result, he became a mentor and advisor to many African-American builders who sought his counsel and expertise on developing building plans. Shortly after World War II, his construction company coordinated with the Veteran's Administration to provide training for black veterans, American carpenters, masons, and draftsmen who contributed to the growth of Jacksonville in the 1950s and 60s.

Hutchins became the first president of the United Craftsmen's and Builders Association, as well as was a member of the Jacksonville Chamber of Commerce, the Florida State Business League, and the National Association of Real Estate Brokers. James E. Hutchins died from a sudden illness on May 16, 1970.

The church's present state symbolizes the rest of the neighborhood, a ghost of its former self. Development continues in Brooklyn, threatening to uproot many of the remaining residents left there.

The church is surrounded by empty lots

A Bible on a podium

Many parts of the floor are unsafe to walk on

The building is currently condemned by the city

Left: Looking towards the front doors of the church

Below: The basement of the church

3

THE BUFFALO SOLDIER'S HOUSE

Located in the historic neighborhood of Brooklyn, this home was once home to one of the many Buffalo Soldiers that settled in the area following the Civil War. Back in February 1864, the United States sent troops down to Florida, including three black regiments, to sever Confederate supply routes and recruit black soldiers. Brigadier General Truman Seymour landed troops at Jacksonville, in an area already seized by the Union in March 1862. Seymour's forces then made several raids in the area, seizing several Confederate camps, capturing small bands of troops and artillery pieces, and liberating slaves, all the while meeting very little resistance.

Despite being under orders to not advance deep into the state, Seymour led his troops towards Tallahassee, assuming he would face only the small Florida militia. They were confronted by Confederate troops near Ocean Pond in Olustee, where the Union forces were defeated and retreated to Jacksonville. The United States 54th Massachusetts Volunteer Infantry Regiment and the 35th United States Colored Troops, both composed of black soldiers, were able to repulse Confederate Troops from advancing into the city and possibly prevented the destruction of the Union forces.

Following the war, Confederate veteran Miles Prices purchased a large plot of land just west of the city, had it platted into lots, and sold them to former slaves and soldiers of the United States Colored Troops, later known as Buffalo Soldiers. This area would later be known as Brooklyn, and by the 1880s, it held a population of 1,000 and a few hundred homes and mansions. In 1887, Brooklyn and several other suburbs were annexed by Jacksonville.

By the 1950s, the neighborhood had nearly 6,000 residents. The neighborhood remained primarily residential, but it eventually developed into a commercial and industrial area due to the increasing use of the railway. Construction of the Fuller Warren Bridge cut off the historically black neighborhood, pushing many of the residents out. This slowly led to the decline of the neighborhood, leaving many of the remaining structures in disrepair, such as the Mt. Calvary Baptist Church.

The oldest house in Brooklyn, the Buffalo Soldier's House, was thought to have been built during the Reconstruction era and owned by a former Buffalo Soldier, though its first owner was never documented.

The people of the Gullah Geechee community are direct descendants of formerly enslaved people and have lobbied for a park commemorating the area's history. Saundra Morene, president of the Jacksonville Gullah Geechee Nation Community Development Corporation, has been unsuccessful in getting the Brooklyn neighborhood designated an African American historic district due to not enough interest in the idea among the current residents. She still plans on working on getting the structures there, such as the Buffalo Soldier's House, officially documented and preserved.

Right: The exterior of the house

Below: Much of the inside has collapsed

The living room. You can see a hole in the wall where a fireplace was once located

A room painted pink

Next door is the operating Church of God in Christ temple

Only one house on the block is still occupied

4

LAVILLA SHOTGUN HOUSES

Decades ago, Jacksonville was filled with homes known by many as "shotgun houses." There is a debate as to how these homes got their name. The most well-known theory is that if all the doors are open, you can fire a shotgun cleanly from the back of the house through the front doorway.

These homes were popular in the South throughout the late 1800s up until the 1920s. They were built in such a way as to allow excellent airflow and an increased number of lots on a single street. They were most popular before widespread ownership of automobiles, so many of these houses were located near railroad hubs and factories.

According to old maps, these specific homes were constructed sometime around 1903 and 1912 and were located at 612, 614, and 616 Lee Street before being moved to their present location. Because the city of Jacksonville's directories ignored occupants in predominantly black neighborhoods, the earliest listing for these homes dates to 1919. At the time, 612 Lee Street was occupied by Columbia H. Boger, a widow; 614 Lee Street was occupied by Daniel Redmon, a porter; and 616 Lee Street was occupied by Thomas Taylor, a driver.

The crack cocaine epidemic of the 80s hit Jacksonville hard, especially for those living in LaVilla, resulting in an increase in crime and furthering the decline. According to Mayor Ed Austin, the neighborhood was "nothing but crack houses, prostitution, and crime." In an extremely controversial move, the City of Jacksonville moved forward with the mayor's plan to "revitalize" the neighborhood. The result was the demolition of most of the neighborhood with the exception of just a few structures that were deemed historically significant.

When the plan was implemented in 1993, residents were kicked out of their homes throughout the neighborhood. The city acquired these specific homes, saving them from utter destruction and relocated them to their current location on Jefferson Street in 1999. The idea was that these structures, along with Genovar's Hall, would anchor a block that would serve as a museum to recreate what life was like in LaVilla before modern development. Since then, they have been on a city-owned lot, decaying along with the aforementioned Genovar's Hall.

The three houses have sat on this lot since 1999

Above: The houses sit on the corner of Jefferson and Church Streets

Left: 612 Lee Street, once occupied by Columbia H. Boger

614 Lee Street, once occupied by Daniel Redmon

616 Lee Street, once occupied by Thomas Taylor

The houses continue decaying as the years go by, worsening with the weather

5

GENOVAR'S HALL

Genovar's Hall was built by Sebastian Genovar in 1895 as a grocery store. It is located in the LaVilla neighborhood in Jacksonville and was constructed across the street from Jacksonville's finest bordello, the Hotel de Dream.

The building became the Wynn Hotel sometime in the 1920s. Louis Armstrong preferred staying here when in town because it was on the most active street in Jacksonville. The first floor of the building was occupied by the Lenape Tavern and Bar, one of the most popular jazz clubs in the city. Along with Louis Armstrong, other jazz greats such as Billie Holiday and Dizzie Gillespie played at the Lenape.

In the early 1940s, the Lenape became known as "the rail of hope," where musicians would hang out, waiting for a job. One of the bar's frequent visitors was Ray Robinson, a blind piano player who attended the Deaf and Blind School in St. Augustine before moving to live with a relative just a block away from the Wynn Hotel. He developed his talents playing as a side-man for some well-known performers before becoming a star himself under the name "Ray Charles."

The LaVilla neighborhood fell into decline in the 1960s due to a massive loss of jobs in the railroad industry, and the construction of I-95 which divided the neighborhood. With the end of legal segregation, many residents left to pursue better job opportunities. Those that decided to stay struggled on a day-to-day basis.

The closure of the Wynn Hotel and Lenape Tavern came about sometime in the 1980s during the height of the crack cocaine epidemic, which destroyed the lives of many in Jacksonville. The final nail in the coffin for LaVilla came in the 90s. In a failed effort to redevelop the neighborhood, most of the buildings were demolished and Genovar's Hall was just one of a few buildings left standing. It currently sits on a city-owned lot along with a trio of shotgun houses. An African-American fraternity planned to renovate the building and to operate it as a museum or jazz-themed restaurant. After a decade of work and over $900,000, Genovar's Hall was nothing but a brick shell. The City of Jacksonville currently owns the property with no plans for what to do with it.

The roof has more rooms inside of it, but the windows were removed when the roof was redone

The interior was gutted many years ago

A rainy day at Genovar's Hall

6

THE MONCRIEF ROAD CEMETERIES

Memorial Cemetery is located at the corner of Moncrief Road and Edgewood. It was established in 1909 by Leo Benedict, a treasurer at Benedict and Pollack Co., who would relinquish ownership of the cemetery just two years later in 1911 to the Memorial Cemetery Association.

The Memorial Cemetery Association enlisted the Afro-American Life Insurance Company, the same company that established American Beach, to operate and maintain the cemetery. By this time, Abraham Lincoln Lewis was president of both the association and the insurance company.

In 1936, the Memorial Cemetery Association had expanded to include both Sunset and Pinehurst cemeteries. That same year, the association was disbanded but the Lewis family continued to own the properties privately.

The Moncrief area was well known for its role in Jacksonville's entertainment industry throughout the first half of the twentieth century. By the 1960s, many of the entertainment and recreational businesses had gone out of business. Around this time, residents began complaining that the cemeteries on Moncrief Road were in decline. The Moncrief area today is considered one of the most impoverished areas in Jacksonville with a high rate of unemployment, crime, homicide, and abandoned buildings.

By the 1980s, the Lewis family was having issues maintaining the properties. In 1986, Abraham Lewis' son, James Lewis, signed over ownership of the properties to Memorial Cemetery Incorporation, a local nonprofit. It wasn't long before they ran out of money required for the perpetual care of the cemeteries, and the City of Jacksonville took over the upkeep.

7

SUNSET CEMETERY

Located at the corner of Moncrief Road and Edgewood Avenue, Sunset Cemetery was established in 1917 with land acquired through the Memorial Cemetery Association. Burial plots at Sunset Cemetery cost $15, which many avoided due to the fact that Memorial Cemetery, a much nicer and more established burial place in the community, offered burial plots for just $5 more. Due to this, Sunset Cemetery didn't gain significance until the 1930s.

Right at the entrance to the cemetery is the Craddock Mausoleum, designed with an Art Deco aesthetic in mind with streamlined details. The mausoleum was built sometime in the late 1930s to mid-1940s by James Craddock, known widely as "Charles Edd." Craddock came to Jacksonville in 1921 and established the Little Blue Chip nightclub at the Richmond Hotel on Broad Street. He later moved on to the New Blue Chip, which at the time was considered one of the finest nightclubs in the South.

He garnered a reputation as a philanthropist when he opened a bread line for the needy at the onset of the Great Depression. He would later lose the New Blue Chip nightclub in 1931 but continued to operate the Blue Chip Hotel and a billiard room and cabaret.

In subsequent years, he would own several other businesses including the Charlie Edd Hotel, the Young Men's Smoke Shop, Uncle Charlie Edd's barbershop, and various loan offices and pawn shops. In 1940, he would open the Two Spot nightclub on Moncrief Road which would be known as "the finest dance palace in the country owned by a Negro". The nightclub also played host to many great African-American musicians such as Cab Callaway, Louis Jordan, and Ella Fitzgerald.

Along with the other cemeteries in the area, the cemetery went into decline around the 1960s. Today, the cemetery is in a bad state with massive amounts of overgrowth, trash littered about the property, and headstones smashed or knocked over.

The Craddock mausoleum

The Langley family mausoleum

The grave of Eli Howell, 1893-1969

The grave of Marcellars Edwards, 1917-1970

The grave of Vonzia Maf Northrup, 1948-1971

Many of the graves, like this one, have trees growing near, which destroy the headstones

It's hard to tell from this photo, but the grave here has sunken in, making a small pit

A veteran's gravestone buried halfway into the earth

The gravestone of Clarence Gilley, knocked over onto the ground

A tree growing between to graves. The tree roots are most likely pulling them toward the tree.

Another veteran's gravestone, Edward Jefferson, knocked over

The graves of Minnie and Sam Washington

Despite all the overgrowth, gravestone can be found far back into the woods

The nicer and much cleaner portion of the cemetery

A Styrofoam cross decays among the gravestones

A veteran's grave, Thomas Felix Jr., with another grave behind it buried within the overgrowth

8

PINEHURST CEMETERY

Located at the corner of Moncrief Road and Restlawn Drive, Pinehurst Cemetery was established by the Afro-American Life Insurance Company's Memorial Cemetery Association in 1928. Unlike Sunset Cemetery, Pinehurst catered to working-class and low-income African-Americans.

In 1992, Pinehurst was designated a local landmark along with Sunset and Memorial Cemeteries by the City of Jacksonville. In September 2018, Pinehurst Cemetery served as the catalyst for a $10.8 million plan by Mayor Lenny Curry to restore the city's long-neglected African-American cemeteries, which not only include the Moncrief Road cemeteries but also Old City Cemetery, Mount Olive Cemetery, and Hillside Potter's Field.

Veteran grave markers covered in overgrowth

More grave markers, most of which are for WWI and WWII veterans

Another veteran's grave, Ike Davis

The graves of Charles McGriff and George Cowart, both veterans

Many graves look like this with the markers illegible or faded away, and sunken into the ground.

The grave was smashed, most likely by grave robbers

9

POTASHCORP PHOSPHATE TERMINAL

In early 1966, Occidental Agricultural Chemicals Corporation opened a $3 million automated phosphate rock, triple superphosphate, and diammonium phosphate terminal. The terminal was part of a much larger complex, which included a phosphate mine and processing plant, located 68 miles northeast of Jacksonville in the town of White Springs. It was "Florida's fastest-loaded phosphate rock terminal," with a loading capacity in excess of 3,000 tons per hour.

Located at the terminal were six concrete storage bins, each 40 feet in diameter and 110 feet high, each holding approximately 5,000 tons of phosphate in storage for export; a car unloading facility, which handles two 100-ton hopper cars at a time unloading on a 48-inch conveyor belt, carrying material directly to a loading ship or to the storage bins at the rate of 2,000 tons per hour; and a mooring facility. Six steel storage tanks would be built much later, able to hold a total of 13 million gallons of phosphoric acid.

In 1995, Potash Corporation of Saskatchewan Inc. purchased all the outstanding shares of White Springs Agricultural Chemicals Ltd. from Occidental for $291.5 million. This included the terminal and its related White Springs mining operations. Just four years later in 1999, Potash Corp. shut the Jacksonville terminal down and consolidated its phosphate export distribution system through Morehead City, NC, which was said to serve its global customers more efficiently and economically.

Not much has happened since its closure as it sits abandoned, waiting to be redeveloped. The area is still visited by those who wish to photograph, and by simple fishermen. Among local urban explorers, it has been nicknamed the "echo domes" for the almost otherworldly echoes the tanks create.

Above: On top of the concrete bins

Right: View from up top at the echo domes

On top of the concrete bins looking towards the river

The concrete bins used to store phosphate

Right: The exterior of one of the domes, red due to years of rust

Below: These are called the "echo domes" by local explorers due to the sounds they create

Left: The size of the domes demonstrated with people for scale

Below: The domes make for some interesting photos

10

JACKSONVILLE FORD MOTOR CO. ASSEMBLY PLANT

Henry Ford founded the Ford Motor Company on June 16, 1903, with $28,000 in cash from twelve investors, most notably John and Horace Dodge, who had founded their own company just a few years prior. During its early years, the company produced just a few cars a day from its factory in Detroit, Michigan. Between 1903 and 1908, Ford produced the Models A, B, C, F, K, N, R, and S, most of which sold in the hundreds or few thousands a year. In 1908, Ford introduced the mass-produced Model T, which sold in the millions.

Inspired by Packard's assembly plant in Detroit, Henry Ford commissioned Albert Kahn Associates to design Ford's Highland Park plant. Along with his younger brother Julius, they developed a new style of construction where reinforced concrete replaced wood in factory walls, roofs, and supports, providing better fire protection and allowing large volumes of the unobstructed interior.

The Highland Park plant was completed in 1910 and included offices, a power plant, and a foundry. It was the largest manufacturing facility in the world at the time of its opening at over 120 acres, and with its spacious design, it set the precedent for future factories and plants.

On October 13, 1913, the High Park Plant became the first automobile production facility in the world to implement the moving assembly line. Due to the new assembly line, it cut the production time of the Model T from twelve hours and eight minutes to just an hour and a half. This also allowed them to lower the cost of the Model T from $700 to just $350 by 1917, making it a very affordable automobile for many Americans.

Due to rising demand, Ford commissioned Albert Kahn to design the River Rouge Complex in Dearborn, Michigan. Being 1.5 miles wide by 1 mile long, it was the largest manufacturing facility after its completion in 1928. Wanting to spread out his investment as well the growing demand for vehicles, Kahn was also asked to design seventeen smaller satellite factories throughout the world, including one in Jacksonville, Florida.

In 1923, the former Bentley Shipyards property was purchased from the city of Jacksonville at $50,000. Construction began on the 115,200-square-foot, $2-million complex on January 23, 1924, and was completed in just six months. The complex included a powerhouse that contained two 225-horsepower boilers and a river-fed 75,000-gallon water tower which was built for the sole purpose of combating fires. The front of the building housed a parts department and its own showroom for finished automobiles.

In an effort to keep up with demands, 50,000 square feet was added to the east side on November 13, 1926. By 1927, the plant had produced nearly 75,000 automobiles, and nearly 15,000 trucks.

The Model T was replaced with the new Model A in 1928, and the plant was retrofitted to begin production of the Model A. Operations continued as normal until 1932 when the Great Depression made it so smaller satellite plants weren't needed. Ford continued using the building as a parts distribution center until 1968.

Throughout the years, the building became home to various companies, including a European-import firm, and a van conversion business. Eventually, it became nothing more than a storage facility, most recently for a wooden pallet manufacturer.

In February 2015, 35 acres next to the Mathews Bridge, including the old Ford plant, was purchased by Amkin Hill Street LLC for $4.4 million. According to the previous owner, while Amkin's manager operated out of Miami, the family is based out of Madrid, Spain, and invests in properties around the world. There are currently no plans for the property.

The factory is guarded by security cameras

The Mathews Bridge can be seen in the background

Inside the immense factory

11

W. P. SUMNER COMPANY

Once part of Jacksonville's Ward Street red light district, this brick structure was constructed in 1910 for the W. P. Sumner Company. The company was first founded in 1887 by William and Alberta Sumner as a grocery store mainly dealing with butter and cheese. When William died in 1900, their son, Charles, took over the business. On May 3, 1903, Sumner's business was destroyed along with over 2,360 buildings during the Great Fire of 1901.

The business was reopened on Laura Street where it quickly grew, leading to the need for a larger facility. This is when the four-story brick building on Ward Street would be constructed. Sumner operated a six-ton ice plant on the first floor, the second floor was used for cold storage, and the third and fourth floors were used for dry storage. While the manufacturing operations were located in the four-story structure, the business' retail was done through the connected single-story building.

Charles Sumner died in 1915 and his business ceased operations as well. A number of small businesses would occupy the buildings until 1920, when it would be occupied by the J. R. Berrier Ice Cream Company. By this time, Ward Street had been renamed Houston Street, and what was the city's red light district was now filled with retail stores and wholesale businesses.

Jefferson Richard Berrier had a sketchy history, both as a businessman and as a person. He operated his ice cream company until 1929 when he sold the business to Foremost Dairies. He went back into the ice cream business in the late 1930s, operating a company in Jacksonville and another in Richmond, Virginia. While setting up the company in Virginia, Berrier's brother was accidentally electrocuted when testing the switchboard which was being installed, killing him. Berrier refused to pay out his late brother's workmen's compensation to his wife.

In the early 1950s, with nearly 100 accounts, Berrier decided the ice cream business wasn't profitable anymore and stopped delivering to those accounts. This resulted in the loss of all but only a handful of accounts who were willing to pick up their goods from the plant. When questioned by the Federal Trade Commission, he claimed his business had declined due to competition from larger companies such as Velda Farms, Foremost, and the now-defunct Borden. He later recanted his statement and simply explained he was out of town too much to properly take care of his business.

Even though he was no longer in the ice cream business, Berrier continued to operate soda fountains in various locations in Jacksonville. In 1961, his business was picketed by the National Association for the Advancement of Colored People (NAACP) due to his refusal to hire any African-American girls as waitresses. The picketing ended when a judge declared the picketing unlawful, as it was accompanied by threats and intimidation of customers.

Back to 1924, Berrier moved out of the Houston Street building and Gray-Von Allmen Sanitary Milk Company moved in. The building was once again vacated during the Great Depression and sat empty until the Cunningham Furniture Company began using it for shipping its products. Cunningham Furniture Company was once one of the largest home furnishing businesses in the Southeast and Florida's oldest furniture company. In 1936, Galinsky Plumbing would be the building's next tenant, using it to store supplies and plumbing fixtures, and would operate out of there until the business' closure in 1983.

The 1980s saw a number of restaurants come and go until 1992 when JoAnn's Chili Bordello opened. JoAnn's Chili Bordello was a small restaurant chain founded by Leonard Doctors and JoAnn Perschel. The restaurant was similar to Hooters, except instead of being a sports bar, it was made to look like an old-fashioned bordello with red velvet, crystal chandeliers, and waitresses dressed up in French corsets and garter belts, and with the motto "seventeen varieties of chili served in an atmosphere of sin." With a history like this, along with the area's former history of being a red light district, it's not surprising how this building is commonly thought of to have been an actual bordello in the past. In that regard, it's interesting to note that the original location on Atlantic Boulevard was a strip club, before and after the restaurant's establishment.

JoAnn's Chili Bordello operated until 2000 when it would be occupied by a couple of bars such as the Sinclair and the Voodoo Lounge. While there were plans to turn it into yet another bar, the building has sat empty since 2012.

A bar counter and shelves are all that remains of the previous tenant

The building operated as an ice cream business in the past

The building has good bones, despite the many years it has been vacant

One of the floors was used for cold storage

Left: The stairwell is a tight fit

Below: Looking towards the front of the building

12

JACKSONVILLE JEWISH CENTER

Next to the Horace Drew Mansion in Springfield lies the old Jacksonville Job Corps Center. The building started out as a synagogue and community center when five orthodox Jewish families got together to form the Hebrew Orthodox Congregation B'nai Israel on December 6, 1901. With just forty members at its start, the membership of the congregation had grown to seventy-five members by 1907. The congregation purchased the lot at the corner of Jefferson and Duval Street in the LaVilla neighborhood for $25,000 and erected a synagogue in its place.

With a growing membership, the congregation hired a rabbi ordained at the Jewish Theological Seminary of America in 1926, who introduced Conservative Judaism and the synagogue-center concept as a means of strengthening and perpetuating Judaism in the community. In 1927, a down payment was placed on a larger site in Springfield and Congregation B'nai Isreal changed their name to the Jacksonville Jewish Center.

Over the next thirty-five years, the Jacksonville Jewish Center expanded its facility to meet the needs of its growing congregation. By 1959, the facility included a two-story sanctuary and chapel, a school, library, gymnasium, meeting room, and office space.

In November 1963, the Jacksonville Jewish Center acquired a property in Mandarin. The following summer, the synagogue's day camp moved to the new facilities which included a recreational park with an Olympic-sized swimming pool and playing fields. The facility is still in use today.

Three years after the Jewish Center relocated to Mandarin, the Labor Department bought the property for $400,000 and opened it in 1979 as the Jacksonville Job Corps Center to train and educate high school dropouts. The Corps operated at this site for twenty-six years before moving to a new location in 2005. The property was bought in 2006 with plans to turn it into luxury housing, but the recession put a halt to any plans.

On April 25, 2011, a fire broke out in the main sanctuary, prompting officials to demolish the building. Neighbors believed that it was the homeless who were using the building for shelter that started the fire. Two buildings remain on the property which includes a dormitory building and the gymnasium/auditorium.

In 2015, the property was bought once again by a developer with plans to build a mixed-use apartment complex on the site. The plans called for demolishing a vacant dentist's office next door and restoring the facades of the two historic buildings left on the property. The gymnasium building would be converted into thirty-four residential units with commercial space on the ground floor facing towards Klutho Park. The dormitory would have been converted into sixteen apartment units. Those plans never materialized and the property remains vacant.

The old signage for the Jacksonville Job Corps still hangs on the front of the building

Looking at the security booth and the front entrance to the right

Left: The building was closed around the holidays

Below: Damage from the fire that occurred in 2011

Above: How the gym looked before it was used for storage

Right: A poster with points for the various Job Corps Centers in the South

An empty office area

One of the many office rooms in the building

Above: More plywood and building materials in the hallway

Right: Inside the security booth

People have recently gotten into the building and vandalized the interior

The gymnasium is entirely filled with boxes of plywood and other building materials

13

FEDERAL RESERVE BANK OF ATLANTA, JACKSONVILLE BRANCH

Now known as the Physician and Surgeon Building, the old Federal Reserve Bank of Atlanta located on Hogan Street was opened in 1924. The building was designed by Henrietta Cuttino Dozier, considered the first female architect in the state of Georgia and the first woman in the Southern United States to receive formal architectural training from a national school of architecture.

Born in Fernandina Beach in 1872, Henrietta C. Dozier was the third and last child of Henry Cuttino Dozier, who died a few months before she was born, and Cornelia Ann Scriven Dozier, both originally from South Carolina. She had a brother, Scriven, and a sister, Louise.

From an early age, Henrietta knew she wanted to become an architect, and after high school, she apprenticed in an architect's office before spending two years at Pratt Institute in Brooklyn, New York. She then went to the Massachusetts Institute of Technology, from which she graduated with an architectural degree in 1899. She was just one of three women in a class of 176, and the only one to graduate. In 1905, she would become the first Southern woman to be accepted by the American Institute of Architects

Henrietta Dozier worked in Atlanta for thirteen years before moving her practice to Jacksonville in 1914 where she became the city's first and foremost female architect. In 1903, she designed the All Saints Episcopal Chapel in Atlanta. Considered her favorite commission, this small chapel was later damaged by fire and incorporated into a larger structure. While still in Atlanta, Henrietta C. Dozier was responsible for the design of the Saint Philips Episcopal Church in Jacksonville, which was constructed in 1903.

She worked for the Jacksonville Engineering Department during World War I and then went out on her own, opening an architectural practice in 1918. During this time, she used various gender-neutral or male-sounding variants on her name throughout her career, including "H. C. Dozier" and "Harry" Dozier. Some of the more noted buildings designed by Henrietta C. Dozier in Jacksonville include the Lampru Court Apartments, which were demolished in 2007, residences at 1819 Goodwin Street, 2215 River Boulevard and 1814 Powell Place, and of course the old Federal Reserve Bank, which was designed in association with Atlanta architect, A. Ten Eyck Brown. She died in 1947.

The Federal Reserve Bank of Atlanta is the sixth district of the twelve Federal Reserve Banks of the United States. Referred to as the Atlanta Fed, it covers the states of Alabama, Florida, and Georgia, the eastern two-thirds of Tennessee, the southern portion of Louisiana, and southern Mississippi as part of the Federal Reserve System. Along with its Atlanta headquarters, it operates five branches with the sixth district, which are located in Birmingham, Jacksonville, Miami, Nashville, and New Orleans.

The Jacksonville Branch was located here on Hogan Street until 1952 when a newer building was constructed. That building is currently occupied by the Jacksonville Fire & Rescue Department. An insurance company, United States Fidelity and Guaranty Company, occupied the building in the 1960s. Dr. Paek Naykoon purchased the building in 1982 as his primary care clinic, which is where it got its current name.

The building was designed in the neo-classical style and the exterior has remained unchanged throughout all these years. However, the interior has undergone vast renovations which have destroyed much of the original work.

Above: The second floor was added during a renovation, possibly in the 70s

Right: One of the offices on the second floor

A bathroom decorated in cheap marble

Another office located on the second floor

Above: With the massive amounts of renovations done in the past, it makes you wonder what's hiding under all the drywall and drop ceilings

Right: Thankfully, no drop ceilings were added to hide the trimmings

Above: The third floor of the building

Left: An office on one of the upper floors with serious water damage

Right: The fire exit, which leads to a fire escape

Below: The front entrance of the building

Left: Part of the waiting area on the ground floor. The words at the top read "Physicians & Surgeons Building"

Below: One of the offices on the ground floor

The front lobby of what is now known as the Physicians & Surgeons Building

A former X-ray room

The basement of the bank

Power still runs through the building, with just this single light on

Right: The building was designed by Henrietta C. Dozier and A. Ten Eyck Brown

Below: The abandoned Jones Bros Furniture Co. building can be seen in the background

14

INDEPENDENT LIFE BUILDING

Standing at nineteen-stories and 260 feet tall, the 262,000-square-foot building was completed in 1955 as the headquarters for the Independent Life and Accidental Insurance Building. The early modernist, concrete-reinforced structure was designed by KBJ Architects, who also designed many other high rises in Jacksonville such as the BB&T Bank Building and the Everbank Center. Granite, marble, and limestone were used extensively for the building's interior, and also featured street-level retail along Julia Street and a sky lounge on the top floor.

In 1975, Independent Life relocated its headquarters to newly completed Independent Square. Independent Square is known today as the Wells Fargo Center, also designed by KBJ Architects, and is Jacksonville's second tallest building.

The Jacksonville Electric Authority (JEA) acquired the building in 1976 and relocated its operations there. During the late 1980s, JEA purchased the Universal Marion Building, and by 1990, they had relocated most of their offices from the old Independent Life building. JEA officially abandoned the building in March 1999.

Throughout the years, there has been a bit of interest in purchasing it, but the work needed to renovate such a large structure has been a factor as to why it's still empty. One proposal involved constructing a thirteen-story addition on the east building of the tower, as well as a parking garage.

In October 2019, St. Augustine-based Augustine Development Group bought the former JEA tower intending to develop 140 apartments on the second through eighteenth floors, a grocery store on the 21,000-square-foot ground floor and basement, and a rooftop terrace with a pool, lounge and a high-end sushi and seafood restaurant on the top floor. Construction is planned to begin in the first quarter of 2020.

The main entry into the building

The entire building looks like this

One of the upper floors

Apartments are planned for the building

The building was gutted in a failed renovation plan

The building has been gutted for many years

Left: A dumbwaiter that leads down into the cafeteria

Below: A board that reads "Jacksonville Electric Authority Training Division"

Right: The old U.S. Postal mail chute

Below: The building's cafeteria

Above: An office near the top of the structure

Left: The building's stairwell

A fire pull station

Two explorers hanging on to a ladder at the top of the building

An explorer climbing to the top of the building

The tower takes up almost half a city block

15

YELLOW WATER NUCLEAR WEAPONS STORAGE AREA

Shortly before the United States' entry into World War II, a 2,600-acre tract of land was purchased in western Duval County and construction began on U.S. Naval Auxiliary Air Station, Cecil Field (NAAS Cecil Field). Operating at full capacity during the war, it became the principal war-at-sea and dive-bombing training center for the U.S. Navy and U.S. Marine Corps. It was a pilot's last stop before being assigned to combat in either the Atlantic or Pacific fronts.

At the end of World War II, NAAS Cecil Field was disestablished and then eventually redesignated as Naval Air Station Cecil Field (NAS Cecil Field) on June 20, 1952. The station was rejuvenated as an operating base for fleet aircraft squadrons and air groups, bringing about the "jet age" for Naval Aviation in the Jacksonville area. NAS Cecil Field's growth was accelerated when it was designated a master jet base specifically used for the operation of carrier-based tactical jet squadrons.

It was around this time that the United States and the Soviet Union were stockpiling nuclear armaments in preparation for a possible all-out nuclear world war. The Yellow Water Weapons Department was established at Cecil Field, but its purpose was kept a secret from the general public.

Marines stationed at Yellow Water spoke about security details to an editor of *Leatherneck*, a magazine for United States Marines, which published four articles about the complex in the summer of 1983. According to the articles, "The Pound" as it was called by Marines, was patrolled on foot and utilized surveillance cameras, sensors and searchlights to keep watch along the fences. The security units in the locked area were armed with M-16 automatic rifles, M-10 shotguns, and M-60 machine guns.

There were eighty-nine ammunition bunkers, ranging from small buildings for high explosives to earth-covered bunkers with reinforced concrete doors for the nuclear weapons. They reportedly had elaborate security systems that would sound high-frequency pitches capable of destroying the eardrum or release toxic gases into the air.

The annex remained a secret to the general public until 1985 when two nuclear weapons researchers published a book, *Nuclear Battlefields*, identifying the base as a storage site for 140 nuclear depth bombs, as well as conventional weapons. Unsurprisingly, the Navy never confirmed or denied the storage of nuclear weapons in the Jacksonville area.

Those who knew about the weapons turned a blind eye to it, seeing it as nothing more than just business. Others weren't too happy about convoys carrying nuclear weapons through downtown Jacksonville and over the bridges.

On September 27, 1991, George H. W. Bush announced that all nuclear weapons would be removed from Navy ships and Air Force planes in the first step toward dismantling them. The last of the weapons were loaded onto trucks on October 1, 1993, to be dismantled at the Department of Energy's Pantex Plant in Amarillo, Texas.

Cecil Field was decommissioned in 1999 and turned over to the city of Jacksonville for redevelopment and later converted into Cecil Commerce Center. The Jacksonville Equestrian Center, the Jacksonville Aquatic Center, a community center, a softball complex, and other amenities are on the north side of the base where Yellow Water was located at.

A few structures and the earth-covered bunkers where the nuclear armaments were stored are really all that's left of Yellow Water Compound. Barbed wire fencing still surrounds the area. The foundation for a helicopter landing pad can still be made out with sprigs of weeds poking out of the concrete. Despite that, visitors are still not allowed and those caught there will be considered trespassing.

A building used today for maintenance equipment

Hazardous waste storage building

A pillbox used during training

Dials and switches for a machine used for the complex's water system

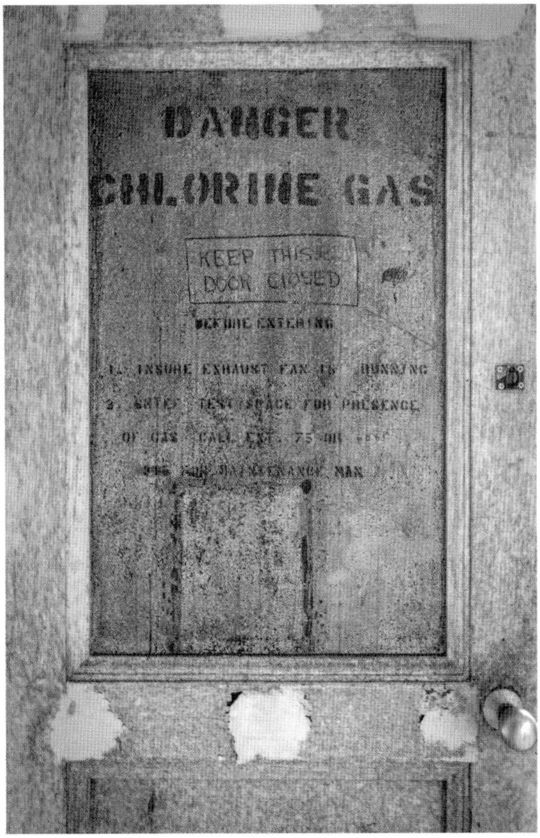

Right: Stencils on a door which reads "DANGER CHLORINE GAS"

Below: An electrical room

One of the few remaining buildings left of the complex

In later years, this warehouse was used by police for training exercises

A sign for cookies and pecan pies

One of the few rooms that had dropped ceilings and carpeting

An empty warehouse

A paint booth for painting vehicles

One of the larger bunkers on the complex

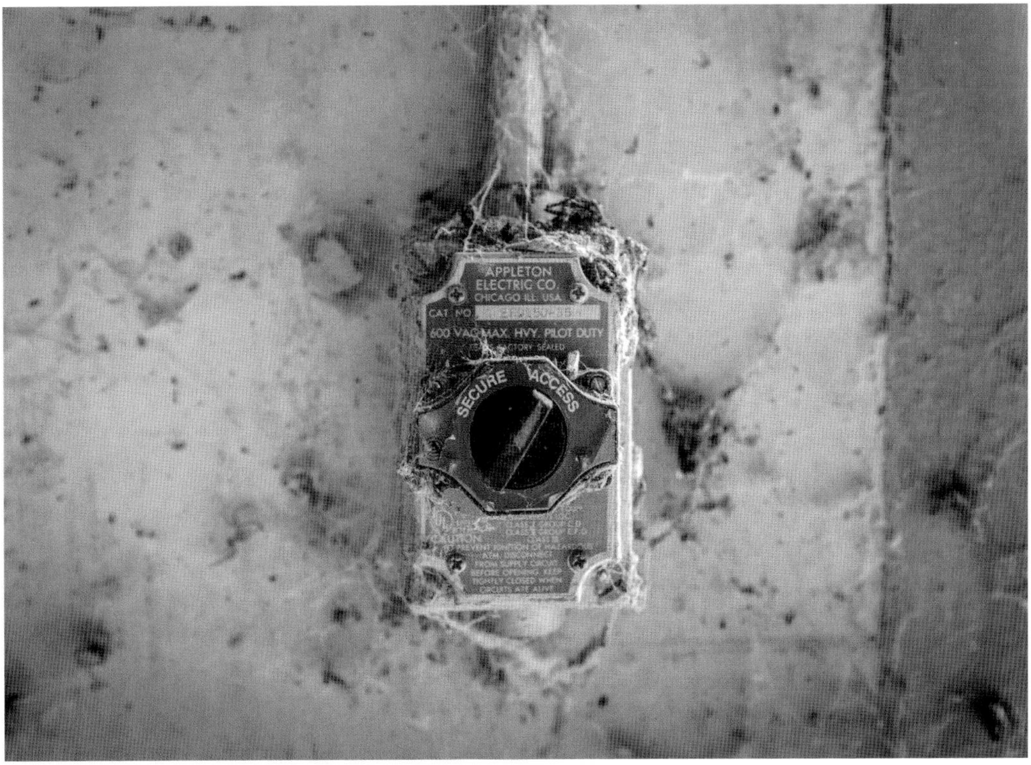

A switch inside of a bunker

Above left: Inside one of the bunkers

Above right: Inside one of the weapon bunkers

Another angle of one of the larger bunkers on the complex

Inside one of the earth-covered bunkers

One of the many earth-covered bunkers used to store weapons

A row of earth-covered bunkers

A long unused guard shack